Get Out Of The Cage:
A Guide To Inner Freedom

Adam Oakley

Copyright © 2014 Adam Oakley.
All Rights Reserved.

ISBN-13: 978-1505246025
ISBN-10: 1505246024

Contents

Introduction – The Cage Isn't Real 1

How To Use This Book 1

PART 1 – GETTING OUT 3

Understanding The Cage 4

No More Maintenance 9

Illusory Bars 22

Cages of Conditioning 30

Let The Cage Crumble 44

Burning The Remains 51

PART 2 – LIFE WITHOUT A CAGE 57

Fellow Humans and Interaction 58

Freedom In Action 68

Free From Strain – Effective Meditation 79

Out Of The Cage and Into Nature 85

On Death and Impermanence 88

Emptying The Collective Cage-Healing The World ..92

Final Words 97

Also Available..99

Introduction – The Cage Isn't Real

The cage is not real. At a certain point we feel as if we are trapped in the cage of the mind – the cage of identity, the cage of obsessive and compulsive thinking, the cage of concepts and ideas, and at a certain point we become sick of it. We seek another way of living, of being. Rather than feeling as if you must fight Life at every turn, perhaps you feel an urge to become free of the many conditioned ways of thinking we have been brought up with. You feel as if Life should not be such an ordeal of suffering, it should not be such a strain or a burden to simply exist. Excellent. Welcome to the book. It aims to point you towards the truth of yourself, and show you that the many ways we have been trained to live and think are false, dysfunctional, and not worth any more support.

The cage of your own mind, is at the end of the day, imagined. It is made of imagination. The person that seems to become caged within the mind, is also imagined. The mental idea of "I am a person" – the personality – is a construct of the mind, that we believe to be who we are. With this belief comes the feeling that you can get trapped in thinking, trapped in dysfunction or negative patterns. The "you" who gets trapped, is just another thought, a self-image.

Just being open to a book like this means that you are already aware of the cage of conditioning and identity, and also have the feeling that you wish to get out. So enjoy the book, I hope it serves in helping you realise that the real you, what you really are, is always out and cannot be trapped.

How To Use This Book

The content of this book is split into passages, each separated by a tree:

Each passage within a tree stands as a pointer within itself, so this book can be very helpful for meditative reading. You may not feel as if you need to read much at a time. Allow for space, for pauses after each passage. Let the words take you deeper.

Once you understand what is meant by the cage (simply the conditioned, personal mind that creates suffering) – this book becomes a helpful guide in that as well as being able to read it conventionally from cover to cover, you can pick it up and read any passage at random.

Take your time with the words, be in no hurry. They all point in the same direction.

Please be aware that words can only point. The thinking mind may wish to get caught up in words and keep your attention in concepts. Let words point, but there is no need to cling to the pointers. To cling to the pointers means you miss what they are pointing to.

I hope this book serves you well in realising your inherent freedom, allowing you to be happy, at peace and effective in the world.

Adam Oakley

www.InnerPeaceNow.com

Part 1 – Getting Out

Who is trapped in the cage? Only who you imagine yourself to be.

Part 1 of this book is about understanding the cage of the mind and how to get out of it.

UNDERSTANDING THE CAGE

What is the cage? The cage is the mind that creates suffering. It is the limited, conditioned, personal mind that can not stop thinking, is lost in time, and creates falsity and delusion. It gives rise to insane habits and behaviours, and creates unnecessary suffering for itself and others. Inwardly it creates unhappy, dissatisfied human beings, and outwardly it creates insane societies that depend on lack and destruction. Addictions to thinking, worry, restlessness, anxiety, sorrow, fear, guilt and resistance are some of the cage's habits.

The cage appears as a personal self who lives in the body. This personal self is not what you are.

The foundation of the cage is who you think you are, rather than what you really are. If we take the cage to be the mind that can not stop thinking and creating suffering, then who is trapped in this cage? The answer may be "me, I get trapped in the cage of my mind". What is this "me"? It claims to represent you – but what is it? It is only a thought – is it not? Look inside – can this seemingly solid person who lives in a body be found? The person who thinks thoughts and suffers the mind – does it exist when you try to locate it?

This idea of yourself has no existence other than in imagination. This personal identity or self-image is the very foundation of the cage.

Our imagination, belief and attention create a personal identity – a person in the head who lives in the body, thinks it is a body, and fears its own non-existence. It suffers pain, enjoys pleasure, and at a certain point feels trapped in thoughts and suffering. Yet it is an imaginary prisoner. This imaginary entity is not who you are, but it pretends to be you. This is what is often called "the ego" in spiritual teachings – the false, mind-made identity.

Whoever you think you are, is not what you really are.

You are the awareness in which the inner person, thoughts, emotions and sensations arise. That is how you *know* thought is happening, how you *know* emotion is moving, how you *know* personal identity is arising – all arises and falls in you. Be aware of this yourself – even if the mind is turbulent, how do you know? If the body and mind is suffering pain – how do you know? The awareness itself is unaffected and ever present. The only confusion that has arisen is identification with objects in awareness, rather than simply being awareness itself.

Believing in the inner person, believing in the mind-made self, is what gives limiting thoughts their power. It charges thoughts and emotions with identity and ownership. To act as if you are no-one, to be empty of concepts about yourself, is to remove the foundation of all obsessive and harmful thinking.

Do not take yourself to be any object in awareness. You are not a thing. Things and objects, moods, feelings and thoughts all arise in you, but do not touch you. Since you are not an object, you can not be touched.

You are always awareness. When are you not? Do not be fooled by the mind that claims "I am not free", or "I can not stop thinking" or "I am not there yet". This voice is a liar, it is false, it is not who you are. You are aware of the voice in the head, so how can you actually be the voice? You are awareness, beyond the concepts of achievement or realisation. Just no longer be fooled by the mind that acts as if it is not free.

Beneath the mind-made self is your true being. *Being* can not be seen with the eyes, but only felt from within. Be aware of your own existence, the sense that you exist, the sense "I AM". It is an indescribable, formless feeling of simply being. This beingness is not a person or a body. Simply feel it, without expectation. It is your own presence, presence itself, beyond the concept of a person "trying" to be present. It is the still, alive space of Life that is unaffected by thoughts, sensations or emotions, and yet is the source of them, the space in which they play. This is the truth of yourself that the cage seems to cover up.

As soon as you define yourself, as soon as you take yourself to be some thought or concept – you limit yourself. Even the word "awareness" can become a cage when it is clung to as only a concept. Any thing you identify with – such as thoughts, emotions or objects – become cages. They are fine in themselves, but why identify with them? Let everything be as it is, inside and out, but do not take yourself to be anything you can perceive – including the body.

The cage of the inner person and its associated thought patterns seeks to maintain itself. It requires your belief for its own survival. It must continually generate noise and enhance a sense of dissatisfaction and separateness in order to be maintained. Simply be aware of its behaviour – the need for the mind to continuously think, the need for the mind to feel unsatisfied, to constantly look outside for pleasure, to always propose that fulfillment lies in the future, to always enhance its own identity by forming conceptual identities for "me" and "other people". When you are aware of this happening, you are also aware that these behaviours are not who you are. In your simple noticing, without judgement or effort, the power of these mental habits are weakened.

Be aware that your mind creates an illusory world of imagination – a world of concepts, memory and interpretations – that is often taken to be the reality of things. What causes you such disturbance is often the inner world of thoughts *about* the outer world, rather than the outer world itself. Experience the sense-perceived existence without believing the addition of the imaginary world of the personal mind. The psychological world of persons, events, opinions and time is a tremendous limitation masked by complexity. The world of human names and labels is an illusion.

A popular theme in spiritual teachings is "self-realisation" – to know what you really are. When you see that the search for your true self takes place in the awareness that you already are, the search is over.

No More Maintenance

Let us no longer maintain the cage of personal identity and its associated limitations and sufferings. Personal identity can be a helpful tool in the world, but when you believe the personality is the truth of who you are, it can become a burden.

The cage requires maintenance, and is maintained by thinking and resistance. That is why it can seem so difficult to not think. "I can't stop thinking!" is the voice of the cage. Who you are does not think – thinking arises in you.

When the person who lives in the head speaks, judges, speculates or commentates – listen to him or her impartially, without opinion or preference. Then it will be clear that the person speaks, while you are listening.

"But I really feel like I get dragged into thinking and can't stop" – attention can get dragged into thinking, yes. But are you the attention? Are you not aware of the attention moving here and there, in and out of the mind? If so, you must be beyond attention.

Do not identify with attention. Attention is merely the surface spotlight of your being. You are the unseen being in which the attention is moving.

The attention gravitates towards the mind habitually of course. You can be aware of the pull of the cage of the mind, and be aware of the attention being pulled. In this way you feel yourself to be beyond attention, and the attention can more easily rest in the awareness that you are.

Simple awareness of the breath is a very useful tool to keep attention and support out of the cage. Even if thinking is going on, being aware of the breath means you no longer become lost in thinking.

In fact if you forgot everything about spirituality or the mind, and just remained aware that the body is breathing – you may be amazed at the results. The only thing to be aware of is that the mind despises attention to be taken away from it, and so it will at first create pain, boredom or negative thoughts to try to distract you. Do not judge or resist this, allow it, and remain simply aware of the breath.

Only being aware of the breath will enhance your awareness of the cage itself – the energy field of the mind, the personal identity that craves thinking. You don't have to do anything about this. Your natural awareness of it is enough. Stay with the breath, and notice that breathing happens by itself.

Another way to remove attention from the mind is to realise that the thoughts that come with obsessive or compulsive thinking are illusions. They are like dreams. The mind's events, fears and identities for yourself and others - are creations of thought - limited interpretations of reality. How can you be sure that any of these thoughts are true? Is it not possible that, like dreams, they are not real, and do not represent true reality? For instance, if you ever think of a person or an event - this is not a true representation of the person or the event. It is in fact a complete creation of the mind, posing as a representative of the reality.

So lose your interest in thought constructs, they will be there when required, but you need not be a slave to them. What do you know for sure, if you remove all past conditioning? You are sure that you exist. So simply be aware of your own existence. Let this be an anchor for your attention. This is sanity, not selfishness, simply be aware of your own existence. In this way you begin to see that the mind arises, speaks and falls of its own accord, it is not your business. The deeper sense "I AM" is always present, and is not a person or a body. It is your real being. It is one with inner stillness or inner space - the emptiness of *being* in which all thoughts and sensations come and go.

Notice the mind's tendency to imagine. Thinking about other people, yourself, events of past and future – all of this is imagination, it is all a creation of thought.

Be aware of the inner space beneath thoughts, the stillness that allows thinking to happen, but is unaffected. You *are* this unaffected space. The self-image that arises out of it is only another thought.

Some common behaviours of the cage-like human mind are: wanting things to be different, and trying to escape this moment. Whether it is useless repetitive thoughts, replaying past events, anticipating future events or intense psychological suffering, the basis is always the same – the mind wants things to be different, and so tries to escape the Now. "Things" can be anything from thoughts, feelings and emotions, to people or circumstances. When you resist what *is*, you maintain the cage.

It seems normal to want things to be different. Particularly if faced with pain or a situation that does not fit in with your mind's expectations, it seems natural to internally resist.

It also seems normal to escape the Now, since if you directly look at the present moment, there is no food for the mind, the mind says this moment is boring, not enough, or empty. Indeed it is empty, but don't believe in the mind's aversion to emptiness.

As an experiment, try not wanting anything to be different. Don't interpret anything, let everything be as it is at this moment. This is called surrender, non-resistance to Life.

How does it feel to not want things to be different, to allow things to be as they are? To no longer need to follow some imaginary circumstance and become lost in a mental movie, to no longer resist how you feel, to no longer resist what thoughts are arising? Is there not a spaciousness, an emptiness that is at peace and alive within you?

This is the space of creativity and of *being*. While the logic of the cage is that all useful action and change can only come from resistance, "since resistance is the only possible motivator for change", through surrender you access the truth of Life, the source of truly useful and creative action. From here you can still get a job, go to work, run a business etc., the only difference is that you enjoy it more, and your action is more effective.

Through surrender, you experience Life directly, purely, not through a filter of conditioning. The cage is no longer upheld through resistance, so you also become aware of your deeper being – Life itself, beyond personality and untouched by time.

If thoughts arise, this does not mean they are true. "I am not free of the mind" is one of the most dishonest thoughts. This "I" *is* the mind. Imagine a liberated being who one day believed a thought that said "I am bound". Then this liberated being would feel bound, when in reality they are liberated. This is what has occurred. Our sense of separateness and inner entrapment are purely imagined and then believed in.

A common spiritual practice is to relax, and simply be a witness to thoughts. To passively observe thoughts, without judging them or getting involved with them. This can be very helpful, particularly in a surrendered, non-resistive state, when you have no conceptual goal in mind. It shows that thoughts are not who you are, they come and go in your awareness.

To go to the root, you can try this: rather than being aware of the thoughts that arise, be aware of the initial desire to think. Simply be aware of the root of compulsive thinking – which is the mind's urge to create thoughts. Be aware of it, that is all.

In this awareness, you are no longer identifying with the desire of the mind to create useless noise. In this way, the urge for constant thought loses its power, and it becomes clearer that beneath the thinking mind, there is a stillness that is naturally at peace.

Whenever the mind interprets what happens through adding thoughts, you rob yourself and the moment of freedom. In an attempt to understand, the mind creates a false understanding. It then creates a mental world, made of pure imagination, and true perception is cloaked in the illusion of thought. Simply perceive without labeling your experience. Allow it. When you leave Life alone, give it freedom to be, you are blessed with freedom in return.

Since the cage is not real, everything it speaks is false. It has hypnotised the whole world into believing its thought systems of resistance, time and separation are true. In fact it has everything upside-down.

As an experiment, see how it feels to no longer believe in the thoughts that arise. You have the right. The power lies with you.

To not believe in thoughts that arise may be labeled as insanity. The world does not understand sanity, however. A common turn of phrase to indicate insanity is "you're out of your mind". To be out of the mind is to be sane. Disregard what you have been told about yourself and about the world, and turn towards the wisdom within, the natural intuition that lives in *feeling* rather than thinking, let creative action arise spontaneously from inner stillness. Thought then becomes fresh, creative and insightful when required, rather than being stagnant, dominating and judgemental.

No longer be a slave to thinking. If thinking is arising, that is fine, it is part of the moment. Your apparent slavery comes only when thought is believed, and you allow it to disturb you. Remain undisturbed and un-knowing.

If thoughts or conceptual knowledge are required, they will be there. You need not carry around rehearsals, mental baggage or dependence on time. Let yourself be empty, so natural intelligence can make use of the body and mind.

We believe constant thinking helps us. It only helps the mind preserve its false identity. A cup's use lies in its empty space. The same with the mind. Dependence on thinking clogs up the tool and makes it the master. Don't depend on thinking to know anything or be anything.

It is far easier to relinquish the addiction to thinking when you surrender your need to understand. Be pure, innocent and unknowing. When you claim you know something, innocence is lost and the cage can once again take footing.

We often speak about the cage of the mind-made self as if it is real. It is only imagination. No need to fear it or take it seriously. In fact, seeing its futility as a kind of funny joke can quickly disarm its hold and withdraw the power of belief.

Be grateful if life is exposing that your judgements are incorrect. Then you can give them up quicker.

No-mind is death of the false. Death of the illusion of separateness. This is why the cage resists silence so much. Let the ego cry out, let it dissolve whenever the universe wishes.

Don't try to obliterate your mind. The cage has then come back. Let it be, give it to God, let Life deal with it, show no more interest.

Truth is non-conceptual. You are non-conceptual. A bird does not call itself a bird. The sea does not call itself the sea. Be done with the mental world of illusions. See things as they are.

A false assumption is that not thinking will mean no action. Action is actually more effective. Because of its efficiency – energy is not wasted, and so action may be less strenuous and perhaps less frequent compared to a body possessed by a restless and fearful mind.

Another false assumption is that without thinking, your life will fall apart. Not true. With a quiet mind, there is less egoic interference, and instead the natural harmony of one's Life can unfold. Sometimes on the surface it can feel as if things are falling apart. This is ok, it is merely an outer reflection of the old conditioned thought patterns dissolving. It must happen so that a new experience of the world can emerge that reflects your natural state of lightness, ease and abundance.

Without constant thinking cluttering up your inner space, the non-conceptual intelligence of Life has more space to enter your existence and take charge with far greater power and harmony that the little ego. Relinquish your judgements of Life and let it sort itself out.

Our parents and teachers are usually all run by the mind that is obsessed with content, with form, with things. Content is given the upmost importance, and everything takes on a heavy kind of meaningfulness. Everything seems to matter so much. Content is temporary, yet we give the temporary things more importance than that which is permanent. Permanence is overlooked, as if it does not exist. This is not how it has to be.

Be aware of this moment itself, rather than what arises within it. The true meaning of the present moment is not the form, it is not "what happens". The moment itself is beyond form.
    The present moment is that formless field in which all content changes. Therefore, this moment never changes, only content changes. Be aware of this "field of Now", and how it

is unaffected by what happens. It lets everything happen. Be aware of who you are in relation to this field of Now. Where is the separation? The separation is only a thought, rather than who you are.

The field of Now is most easily experienced when you are not resisting the moment and its contents. Allowing the contents to be as they are, without creating judgements or interpretations, means that the form no longer takes on such a huge importance or solidity, and you are aware of the underlying force of Life, creative and untouched.

Be aware the conditioned mind does not want freedom. Freedom and inner nonresistance are its end. Be aware that something resists freedom, even if you feel you wish to be free.

Yet who wishes to be free? Only the mind. You are already free as awareness of the mind and all else.

The same personal mind that meditates and practices, sometimes for years, is the very reason for apparent bondage. So the mind seeks freedom and peace, when it itself is what creates the opposite.

If inner freedom could be described, one description could be: the seeing that whoever feels trapped, is not real, and that there is no one inside who can be trapped or harmed. The personal self is only a mind-made fiction.

The reason we seem to suffer our minds so much, the reason it seems to be so powerful is because we give it so much credit. We give all power away to it by being fascinated with it, believing it, and being dependent on our minds to be a certain way before we can be happy or at ease. If you didn't believe in the mind, it would not exist for you. This is how powerful your belief is. Many thoughts could come, but if you did not believe them, they would not disturb you.

Don't give credit where it's not due. Don't be an inner slave to voices and images. You are beyond them. Give awareness to yourself. Feel the presence that permeates the body. Surrender any expectation or resistance. The mind will sort itself out when you no longer try to manage it or support it.

The cage only seems real when you believe in it.

Who do thoughts actually affect? Thoughts can only trouble other thoughts. Some thoughts come along and make other thoughts react. You are beyond all of this. Let thoughts play, never resist the mind. In this nonresistance you are aware of a stillness or emptiness beneath the mental noise, felt at first within the body, that is untouched by thoughts or emotions. This stillness is not separate from yourself. It feels separate when we believe we are the cage of "me" – the personal mind that arises out of the stillness. Simply no longer take yourself to be any object, including the mind-made "me" which claims to think, suffers thoughts and wishes to be free. We are quick to identify with objects, rather than knowing ourselves as the nothingness out of which they arise.

Part of spiritual conditioning is that you can only be free of the mind after years of meditation or living in a cave, or that you must search and have some monumental experience. These are false boundaries. Just stop believing in the mind's interpretations of reality. Job done.

Illusory Bars

We keep the cage intact when we continue to identify with old mental habits and beliefs that seem to keep us trapped. Really they are just imagined, and have no meaning. Often the mind can throw these up most strongly when it is at its weakest, when you are no longer supporting it. These include:

The Belief "I Am The Body, I Am A Person, I Am My Thoughts"

You are that in which the body, sense of personality and thoughts arise. Without you they would not exist. When you say you are them – these are just more thoughts. You exist when no thought is there, and you exist when thought is there. It is more truthful to simply say: you *are*.

The natural sense of being, or "I AM", has identified with the mind and conditioning. This creates a small, separate identity that believes it is a body and a thinking mind. This form-identity arises in your awareness, so how could it be what you are?

Fear Of Not Knowing

"Without thought, I will not know anything" – this can be a fear that the mind throws up. Welcome this fear, but see it as meaningless. The mind creates a false knowing through concepts and past conditioning. Whatever it thinks it knows, is not true, and only really serves to sustain itself and your dependence on it. Without thinking, you move into a deeper understanding of Life, one that doesn't need a constant inner commentator.

FEAR OF DYSFUNCTION OR NO ACTION

"But without thinking I will not be able to get anything done, how can I still act in the world?" – of course this is the mind speaking. It has taken over the role as the "doer" and sees itself as totally responsible for all actions of the body. Action still occurs, but with less sense of doer-ship. This actually makes action more effective, since it is not weighed-down with attachment or personality.

Who beats the heart, breathes the air, digests the food? Is there any person responsible for maintaining these most basic and fundamental actions of Life? If we are not personally responsible for these most basic things, why do we think everything that comes later is our own burden to bear? Does Life not have an intelligence of its own, to which the personal mind is merely a tool?

FEAR OF DEATH

Without maintaining the cage, gradually you may feel your

old conditioned identity slipping away or weakening, as if you are not "you" anymore. The "you" that can disappear, is not who you are.

"I feel as if I'm dying" – says the ego. Yes, in a way the ego is dying. The cage of the limited, illusory self is diminishing. The self that claims it is an object, is dissolving, to reveal what is true, but is not an object. It is what you are. The real Self.

BELIEF **I**N **T**HOUGHT

As mentioned earlier, belief in thought is what keeps it strong. We have been trained to believe in every thought that arises, without doubt. So we end up believing in what is not true, and doubting what is real and unchanging. Our faith has gone in a false direction. You need not believe any thought. How can you be sure that any thought is the truth of reality? Is it not more accurate to say that no thought can be true, since each thought is a limitation, attempting to interpret the infinite and incomprehensible?

Without belief in thinking, the mind will still be there when it is required for practical use, but it will no longer be a hindrance or an interference. It becomes a tool rather than a master.

If you believe "these are my thoughts", then they will hold more power, since the mind loves to possess. If you see that thoughts arise, and in fact they are not "yours", your attachment will diminish, and so will their power.

BELIEF IN PAST

The past can take charge in the mind – thoughts of what happened, what should or should not have happened, how it would be if it happened differently, what "I" or "he" or "she" should have done – and yet the past is no more. Can you actually locate it other than a thought or feeling? The past is not real. It is imagined. See this clearly – that the past truly is no more, then it cannot command so much attention, belief or interest.

BELIEF IN FUTURE

Where is the future? We act as if we know what will happen, and this false knowing is based on past experience. It could be said that this is a manifestation of karma – re-living the past again and again. Be done with the past. Don't subscribe to the model of Life that the mind presents through past events. Let it be new, fresh, un-anticipated and spontaneous.

BELIEF IN REHEARSALS

The mind claims that mentally preparing what to say or do when you encounter a situation (usually a social or work-related situation) is of benefit. Have you noticed that when the situation actually arises, things are different, often not how the mind imagined them? If you say what was rehearsed, have you noticed it can feel forced, or just unnatural?

Our belief in the value of mental rehearsals, and our belief in the "inner rehearser" is what can keep us feeling trapped in time and worry. Whenever an "inner rehearsal" arises – just observe it without getting involved. Let it happen. Let the little voices in the head speak, but show no interest, don't interfere. Then you can see that it is only a mental habit playing out, rather than being who you are. The more empty of rehearsal you are, the more intelligent you will be in real-time, when a situation actually arises. The spontaneous intelligence of Life takes over. Put down your baggage.

DESIRE TO UNDERSTAND

Thought offers to help us understand things "better". Really thinking helps us understand things less, since we just keep adding more and more concepts to things that are beyond mental understanding. Don't act as if you wish to understand anything. Allow yourself to be empty and un-knowing. Then you access the source of true intelligence and non-conceptual understanding.

DESIRE FOR MORE

More thoughts, more understanding, more events, more experiences, more satisfaction, more identity – all these desires support an addiction to thinking. Give them up and see how it feels.

DESIRE FOR IDENTITY

Thinking upholds the false self, the conceptual "me". The "me" desires to be preserved and maintained. Therefore it fears and resists no-thought. Act as if you have no desire to be anyone or anything. Don't be a slave to identity.

LOVING THE CAGE'S SECURITY

Whatever inner entrapments there are – provide an element of security. It feels as if we know something, or that we *are* something or someone. The imaginary prisoner actually fears itself and its cage being destroyed.

The cage loves to sustain itself, even if it means feeling trapped and unhappy. Can you be aware of this in yourself? That something loves to feel trapped or un-free?

The cage still provides some degree of perceived protection, some element of security that the imaginary prisoner (the personal self) can survive. The imaginary prisoner fears freedom, since in freedom, it can no longer exist.

<u>Trusting The Mind</u>

We are taught to trust the mind. The mind is seen as the great protector, the fountain of knowledge and the source of all power. It has basically taken the role of God. You may notice that the inner attention takes a slave-like stance towards the mind, constantly being dragged into believing in thoughts.

We then believe in all of the mind's insanity. All the labeling, judgements, fears and idiosyncrasies of the mind are then seen as normal and perfectly sane in our society. Rebel against all of this, without fighting. Take the chance to no longer trust this voice in the head that creates an illusory world of concepts. See that everything, at this moment, is as it is.

Belief and trust in the mind, attention being dragged here and there – you can be aware of these things. So who are you?

CAGES OF CONDITIONING

We have been taught a lot of nonsense. Most of what we have learnt keeps us in limitation, suffering and false identity. So, even for a moment, forget what you have been told, and let this moment be as it is.

First we must remember to not blame anyone for teaching us to think dysfunctionally or within limitations. Everyone only does what they believe to be correct. Rather than society being the cause of mankind's inner dysfunction, our inner dysfunction is the cause of our society. Therefore with a collective increase of sanity, society can not help but shift to reflect this.

We must recognise that the old ways of thinking – the strong belief in time, fear, separation, scarcity and worry – should now be discarded. It clearly doesn't work anymore. Our thinking in this way *creates* corresponding outer realities.

The foundation of society is the mind of human beings. It is now creating misery and maintaining circumstances of suffering. Rebel against the primary teachings of separation and slavery to thinking, by being in touch with who you are before the personality arises. Confirm yourself to be the awareness in which all energies play. Relinquish your personal mask, and be the truth.

We can think clinging to things and being attached to possessions means that this increases our chances of holding on to them.

Have you ever been around a clingy person? Do you want to be with them or do you want to get away? Possessions are no different than people. All is consciousness. If you are less clingy, more open and unprotective, you become more attractive.

We are taught that in control and manipulation there is strength. This is actually weakness. Have you noticed that when trying to control things, you feel very disturbed, dependent and needy?

We are often trained to never be satisfied, to always want more, to overlook what we have and treat it as not enough. Discard this madness. Be grateful for what you do have – not as a mental concept, but as a reality, right now, at this moment, is there any lack? Our minds can make a sense of lack seem far more significant than it really is for most of us.

With surrendered presence comes natural gratitude, for nothing in particular, and yet everything is appreciated. This is the foundation for abundance.

One of the biggest things school teaches is dependence on thought, to have all the answers, that concepts represent truth. It also supports personal autonomy and competition over your classmates. Forget all of this for a moment. Don't look to thoughts to give you anything. Relinquish competition, even with yourself. Let the universe govern your actions.

Self-criticism is a trained behaviour. You may grow up with a concept of yourself that other people criticise, so your mind naturally believes that this is a valid tool or behaviour. We can even believe self-criticism is useful so that we can be better at this or that.

Have you ever tried not criticising yourself? Have you felt the peace that comes with no longer obsessing over being better or anything different? Have you also noticed that in this state, you can still be involved in and work at any craft, improve in skill, but it is even more enjoyable - done from the enjoyment of the task rather than as a means to an end?

You are always told that you are a name and a form - an extreme limitation. Have no name. Have no form. Action will not be impaired, and you can feel yourself beyond apparent limitations.

What you really are cannot be conditioned, conditioning is only for the mind.

We are taught, often indirectly, that inner resistance helps. If anything, it perpetuates undesirable situations and breeds suffering. Most films and TV shows (where we get lots of our ideas about reality) depict people overcoming hardships mainly through resistance. These are the cage's ideals, to show that resistance works.

All that inner resistance actually tends to do is maintain the cage of the personal self. We believe in the power of resistance so much because that is all we have seen. If our society knew the value of not internally opposing the present moment, we would naturally allow a power that sustains creative and useful action to emerge more fully into the world.

We could still say that useful actions have come from resistance. Things have been overcome. But could it be that the common human patterns of resisting Life and making an enemy of the world, are actually creative, contributing factors to circumstances that reflect these habits outwardly? Surrendered humans would create a society where terrible hardship and struggle would not exist – it would eradicate the very framework of society that allows for such injustices to occur in the first place.

Our society makes us believe in competition and scarcity. So we believe that if someone else has something, our chances of getting it are diminished. As if there is not enough to go around. This just isn't true.

If you are happy for someone, welcoming their success or acquisition, you fill yourself with these same feelings of success or acquisition. If you feel jealous and wish someone didn't have or achieve something, then you fill yourself with lack. Then you become respectively attractive or repellant. Truly what you do to others is what you do to yourself.

Something in us often withholds giving, since it does not want to feel diminished by having less. Often it is not things like money we fear having less of, but the ego fears *it* will be less if it owns less.

Then we hear that if you give more you receive more. Then sometimes we force it. We give with the expectation of receiving, and the same lack-mentality remains.

Gradually you relax, you trust, you surrender, and you give freely when the moment requires. This is real giving – naturally, not forced, not expecting anything in return. Then you feel full, without lack, and this is the quality of life that comes back to you as a reflection.

Ownership. How can you own anything? We have tried so hard to make ownership seem real, but it isn't, it is only concepts. Feel the freedom of not owning anything internally. If you own it internally, it also owns you. It controls your moods and happiness. You receive what you give - so if you don't own something internally, it can't own you.

The car is still in your name, you still have a house, but with less "my" or "mine", there is less strain.

Don't be fooled by judgements such as "laziness". This is usually just a term used to make people feel so guilty that they believe it is justified to work harder for companies or governments. It also maintains the cage's mantra: "life is a strain". It has become so extreme that if someone refrains from activity for a time, they are labeled "lazy".

If "laziness" is there, let it *be*. Either it is of use to re-gather energy and strength, or it is something useless. With allowance, acceptance and awareness, what is not helpful will dissolve.

Rudeness, laziness, money, time, days of the week, problems, thoughts, fear, unhappiness - all illusory human creations.

We can often believe to get something, the best way to get it is to feel lack, or to feel closed or negative. We believe these are healthy motivators. Really, whatever makes you feel closed or heavy cuts you off from the flow of Life. So be aware of it and let it *be*, rather than taking it to be who you are.

Most of us get taught a scarcity mindset. We are taught to believe in lack, as if there is not enough, as if the same intelligence that runs nature perfectly is completely separate from us, and we must strive, struggle, fight and worry to survive.

Surrender to this lack mentality, and see that it only consists of imagination. This is enough. Be here without resistance or expectation, and allow your illusions to be undone.

We think our outer world creates our inner turmoils. It is the other way around. Our inner turmoils create the world perceived as outside of us, which then gives false evidence to believe that our inner nonsense and limitations are justified and real. Undo it from the inside with surrender, awareness, non-seriousness, non-belief, allowance. Transform the world from the inside out.

Since many people around us may view Life a similar way –

that the world is very meaningful, serious, ready to destroy you, and justified in creating fear – we can start to believe there is no other way to approach things. There is. Of course there is. You can live without burdensome concern, without worry, without that the heavy layer of seriousness that so many seem to carry without even realising it. You just have to realise that your suffering is mostly created by your own thoughts, rather than the world itself, and that this suffering does not serve a useful purpose. It is purely destructive and dysfunctional, yet claims to be of use.

Obsessive and fear-based thinking can go on unnoticed. It is so normal for society to promote the ideals of lack and scarcity, that often our dysfunctional ways of thinking seem normal and justified.

Be aware that something inside wishes to remain fearful of the future, enjoys to believe in the idea of lack, or the idea that if you do not fight for survival, the world will crush you. Simply notice this, without drawing conclusions. Beneath this noise is the silence of ease and abundance, which knows no fear, and knows no lack. Let this emerge into your life and the world, and it will reflect itself back to you.

We are often taught that Life should be hard, that you are born so that you may justify your existence and earn your place in the world. When we believe it, it seems to be our experience. Question this. Do you really deep down feel as if you are a person limited in power, continually at the whim of the laws of nature, subject to a world that "works a certain way" that dominates your thoughts and actions? Or deep down do you feel that this is not true, that in fact you are beyond all of this, untouched, not at the mercy of anything, and so without need for resistance, trouble or trauma? Whichever is true for you, live from that place.

Effort and struggle are too over-valued. There is a far easier and more effective way of life, which is founded on inner nonresistance. Let life live you rather than you living life.

We are taught to value expectation and attachment. Without expectation or attachment to end results, you allow non-conceptual intelligence to emerge. This intelligence is spontaneous, far beyond the conditioned mind. It knows nothing, yet knows all. It also produces far more effective action than claustrophobic fear-based thinking does.

We are taught to "be someone". We are taught an ideal way to be. This is usually confident and somehow superior to others, be it through salary, qualifications, looks, possessions, or anything else. Instead, feel what it is like to be no-one. Embrace nothingness. Let your identity merge in *being*. This is freedom. Freedom from self and free to be moved by universal intelligence. Then true intelligence can take over your words and deeds.

I remember being told: "you should be worried!". We believe worry is a helpful tool. How much does it help? Does it help at all? How laughable that we can be held hostage by something as useless and self-harming as worry. It is pointless. See it for yourself.

The natural assumption of most, which gets passed on down the generations, is that the world should submit to your will. Things should go your way, and the world should make you happy. If it doesn't, then you should be disturbed or troubled. Where have we got this from? Why should the world conform to the wishes of each little ego? Give the world freedom to be as it is. Then you are also free, as you are.

Competition is useless. Do not compete, do not compare. Then you are free, and able to move with life at the natural pace for your expression, rather than trying to live up to some imagined ideal that has no place in your experience.

Why be attached to success or fear failure? These attachments and fears actually hinder action rather than serving you, so leave these tendencies alone. Carry out action with purity and presence, and the rest will take care of itself.

While we can speak about the benefits of not being attached to outcomes, not desiring "success" or fearing "failure", these tendencies can still live on in us unnoticed. Simply be aware of them, and let them be. They are normal. Don't suppress or resist. Allow them without trying to satisfy or resolve them. Then what is useless is healed, and what is helpful will support action.

Why try to be like anyone else? It is quite unnatural. Of course essentially we are all one, but in terms of your physical life and expression, be guided by your own being and intuition. You need not follow a framework or live by "shoulds" and "shouldn'ts". Live free, without rules or judgements. Your actions will be most effective when you are natural.

Let your reactions *be*. We are also conditioned to believe that "spiritual people" should act a certain way. Let your reactions happen. They may get acted out or they may not. Above all else, do not suppress. If an emotion or reaction cannot be observed and allowed, releasing it through some kind of expression (preferably without damaging anything or anyone else) is more beneficial and healthier than burying it because you think to be "spiritual" you should not show emotion.

Let what happens, happen. In this state you are not resisting, and so reactions cannot dominate you anyway.

Spiritual conditioning may claim that you should always be at peace. Then if we are not at peace, this can generate even more resistance and disturbance. Never say "I should be at peace, I should not be feeling this". Don't deny through resistance, this just fuels discomfort.

Whatever arises, do not identify with it and do not judge it. Let it *be*.

Don't condition yourself. Don't cage yourself by trying to act a certain way or feel a certain way. Freedom is allowing thoughts and feelings to be as they are, without needing to get involved, without depending on these transient sensations for happiness.

Forget the notion that you should be at peace or should be happy, and instead allow yourself to be as you are. In this there is inherent peace, and a happiness that the world rarely speaks of.

The most major conditioning is not how to act, but who you are. Everyone addresses you as a separate person, a tiny fragment in a separate universe. This separate self is a mere speck in the vastness of consciousness. You are the consciousness, not the speck.

Forget the idea that your mind must be silent. The quickest way for the mind to relax is to no longer put conditions on it. Thought itself is resistance, and naturally we identify with the resistance that comes with thought. Allow thought and associated resistance so completely and totally, that it is as if you don't exist, that there is no one who can resist a thought or want the mind to be otherwise.

Don't let this book or any other guide become more conditioning. It is common for spiritual teachings to speak of things like having no desire, not being attached to outcomes, not wanting success or money etc. Then if these desires are inside you, the mind's reaction is to deny them or suppress them. Always allow yourself to feel however you feel. If you feel angry, sad, lonely, bored, happy, joyous or at peace, desiring extreme wealth or desiring nothing, full of lust or full of purity – simply allow it. Allow these things without following after them or being dependent on them. Just allow them to be there. In your allowance of desire, you are not dominated by it since you are no longer desperate to satisfy it. Everything useful then influences your Life, and everything useless is dissolved.

LET THE CAGE CRUMBLE

The cage is ready to crumble. That is why it requires so much maintenance through attention, belief and thinking. Rather than trying to break out by force, you can just give up resistance. The cage *is* resistance, so to surrender and no longer resist what happens, inside or out, is to destroy the cage.

The inner personal cage survives by opposing what is happening and what is experienced. To no longer resist, to relinquish judgements and interpretations, to accept this experience as if you want it, is to crumble the cage, and realise your freedom.

To offer no resistance to Life, to fully allow the experience at this moment, is to go beyond it. Surrender is only to the immediate experience of this moment. With surrender comes peace and transcendence. It also dissolves the resistive energy blocker of the ego, and allows you to become one with what is happening. Your actions are then supported by the moment itself, if action is even required.

The old regime of thinking is to be in opposition to what happens. To resist and fight so that nothing "goes wrong". In this way of living, the purpose of the world is to maintain the cage and its opposition to Life.

The enlightened way is to no longer approach Life with opinions or demands. To surrender, to allow this moment to be as it is. Then the purpose of the world is to destroy the inner cage, which crumbles and dies in the inner climate of nonresistance. So rather than the world being here to make you happy, it is here to wake you up.

Non-resistance does not mean that no action can be taken. It means that action has a higher quality, free from fear and past conditioning.

Surrender is not weakness. The cage says it is weakness – since in surrender, the cage weakens. All of society will support the attitude of resistance and opposition to life, as if you know better than the universe. With surrender, non-resistance to this moment, your separation diminishes and you become one with what happens. Also, you no longer suffer, and the doorway to *being* is opened up.

Surrender is to offer no resistance to the form of this moment. This includes objects, thoughts and emotions. In surrender, you are taken beyond form and abide as formlessness.

Most of our suffering comes from the resistance we support against a situation, rather than the situation itself. The situation is as it is. Be aware that often most suffering comes from all of the mind's thoughts *about* a situation - how it interprets things, what it tells you about what is happening, how it judges and resists - rather than the situation itself, which is beyond labels.

Without using thought, does a situation even exist?

It seems that resistance serves us to take useful action, to change that which is undesirable. Really its main purpose is to maintain the cage, maintain separation, and maintain a sense of unjustness and unfairness in our reaction to Life.

The cage seeks to replace God. It commands, attempts to manipulate, judges and generally tries to control all. Its attempts are mostly futile, and only serve to maintain itself and to increase suffering. Hand your judgements and resistance over to Life, let Life take care of itself - it has enough intelligence of its own, far beyond the comprehension of the human mind.

When you are internally geared towards truth, the outer life conspires to help free you. You may think things are going wrong or life is becoming unfair. Really what is happening is Life really sets out to destroy the inner cage. It keeps shaking up the ego until its resistance and demands become too much for you to bear, and you are forced into surrender, into truth, into peace.

With surrender comes inner peace. This allows the vibration of your body to become higher, more peaceful, more alive. You also feel far less fear, and therefore more love and a natural sense of abundance i.e. a lack of scarcity. This in itself is the foundation for all positive and helpful change in one's life. The universe can work with you since you are allowing its existence. You are no longer rejecting or denying Life, and are therefore supported by it. Since your vibration becomes higher, cleaner, your outer life begins to shift to reflect this.

With surrender your will becomes the universal will. This could be called the will of God. A force far more intelligent than the cage's self-proclaimed knowledge can move into your life more easily and take care of everything.

Inspiration comes most easily to the surrendered, empty mind. When you are allowing this moment without limiting it or yourself into a judgement, you become available for useful and inspired action.

Society teaches you to fear Life, to fight Life, to always have your guard up, as Life will be quick to knock you down. If you believe this lie, then it appears to be true in your reality. Don't act like Life has it in for you. Become its ally – it responds instantly. Welcome this moment without interpreting it. Leave it alone. Let it be.

Why should the world, people and events conform to the wishes of a little ego? What we see in the world's societal and political structures that cause suffering, is a manifestation of the cage demanding its needs be met. It is on a false power trip.

No longer contribute to the madness and futility of constant control. Leave life to Life, let it happen, leave it be. Then you are aware of something in you that is not dependent on anything to be at peace. This is freedom. Without you trying to play God, there is space for the universal force to move more fully into your awareness and affairs.

The whole of Life is your guru. This includes all the people, objects and "events" that take place in it. All are looking to destroy the cage, which is why it feels so afraid. It knows that through your inner nonresistance and neutral awareness, it will crumble. It knows that the outer events that take place will expose it and threaten its existence. Let the cage diminish.

The purpose of the world is not to make it meet your expectations. This is never reliable. Let it destroy what is false about you so you can be free.

This moment has been brought about by Life itself. Honour it, respect it by allowing it to *be*. As a by-product, your connectedness with Life deepens, and Life is experienced with harmony.

Surrender to this moment takes you beyond form without effort. You become aware of that which allows impermanence to *be* – the eternal, formless moment, which is no different than your Self.

One of the biggest obstacles to inner peace is the belief that you should be at peace when your inner state is disturbed.

Instead of trying to be at peace, drop any belief that you should feel any particular way. Don't become subject to spiritual conditioning. Then completely accept your inner experience, as it is, without judgement, responsibility or interpretation.

We often fear our reactions to possible events rather than the events themselves. We do not want to experience the pain of resistance to life that arises in certain situations. Surrender highlights this – the present moment is as it is.

Never fight the mind. It is too well-versed in combat. It has all the moves. Instead fully allow it, let it be. In your openness and allowance, it is made clear that the mind moves while you are aware of it. Without effort, it is seen that you are not the mind, nor anything perceivable.

Burning The Remains

Pain, when allowed, not judged or resisted, will burn everything you are still carrying around inside. When treated a certain way, pain becomes a tool for liberation rather than something that makes you feel trapped and helpless.

Whenever the cage is under threat, it will often throw up pain to distract you, to make it seem as if breaking free is wrong or painful. People sometimes notice that when they become simply aware of their breath – a direct anchor into the present moment and out of the cage of the mind, they feel as if their minds attack them – intense emotional energies flare up. Let this happen, it is not personal. It seems as if the cage fights for survival and becomes uncomfortable. In a sense this is true. At a deeper level, the old pain is bubbling up and being released.

Eat pain. Eating pain means only this: to no longer run from it, to no longer fight it or feel victimized – and to instead surrender, embrace it fully, welcome it, to not label it or interpret it, to accept it as if you had chosen it be there, even treat it as if it is pleasure.

This attitude when facing anything from mild emotional irritation to intense physical pain, is the most effective way to cut the habit of suffering, and even heal the pain.

Complete acceptance and non-judgement of pain will mean you are no longer suffering. It is resistance to pain that hurts most. Let pain *be*.

Pain immediately triggers resistance. Resistance *is* suffering. Let this resistance be as it is.

What is it that suffers pain? It feels like you suffer, but can't the sufferer also be witnessed? Can you be aware of the sufferer? Can the sufferer actually be found as a tangible entity?

The entity that suffers pain is another sensation you are aware of. You are awareness, not the sufferer.

Does awareness suffer? That which can see suffering and is aware of the sensations associated – does this awareness suffer? Is it ever affected by anything?

"I'm in pain!" – who says this? Who is the entity that actually feels as if they are IN the pain? This entity is the false self-image, and is part of the pain itself. In reality, you are not in pain. Pain is in you.

It is not the pain that causes most suffering, it is the natural urge to want the pain to be gone that causes such anguish. If pain is there, reverse the natural resistive response by simply no longer arguing with it. Let it be there, no longer wish it to be gone, even welcome it. This can have miraculous results.

When the initial aversion and resistance to pain have been relieved, you may wish to investigate the pain. What is it? Is it real? Does it have a beginning or an end? Can it be defined? Where does it come from? When you feel pain without resisting it, when you observe it without mental interpretations, it may become clear that the pain is not as solid and tangible as it first seemed.

If any kind of negativity or painful emotion arises within you, notice its futility. When you see that these things do not help, you can let go without effort.

Part of the human condition is to be addicted to suffering. Watch it in yourself without judgement. There is a tendency for an energy field to create inner suffering or trouble, and feed on it, to become immersed in it. We could call this energy field "The Painmaker" – since it periodically seeks to create pain or suffering in oneself or another, and secretly enjoys it.

The Painmaker enjoys emotional pain. Otherwise why is this pain being produced? It believes that emotional pain is helpful. Is it helpful? Once you are aware of this strange addiction to emotional pain, be aware of it, watch it with neutrality, and let it be. Then you naturally break free from it.

When you watch emotional pain in the body without judging it, without labeling it, you realise it is an energy field that has taken root in the body. It is not who you are. As the awareness, you are not affected. So let it create as much pain as it wants. When you fully let it happen, without expecting it to be different, this is where healing takes place.

What a joy to realise that the energy field that seeks to create emotional suffering is not who you are! It takes hold of the mind-made identity, the foundation of the cage, and it infuses related thoughts with energies of pain. See that it is a self-preserving energy field. It is not who you are. If this is seen, its grip will weaken and it will gradually dissolve.

The Painmaker can not maintain activity in an inner state of nonresistance. When you can be aware of pain without wishing it be gone, the conflict and resistance diminishes. The suffering diminishes. Therefore the fuel for the Painmaker diminishes.

You may notice it in yourself or another – that the mind is always looking for something "wrong", it is looking for a problem, something to complain about, judge, or criticise. It often loves to blame others. In many ways, it acts like a spoilt child – kicking up a fuss if its apparent demands are not met.

This serves to maintain the cage of separate identity, and enhance the resistance towards Life, which sustains the cage.

To be free of it, just watch this tendency without judging it. Let it act out, let it play. Through your allowance, it becomes clear that it is not who you are, and so its internal dominance fades.

Treat any pain as if it is pleasure. As if you have chosen it. As if you love it. See what happens.

Part 2 – Life Without A Cage

Without a cage, without an inner person consuming your attention, pure Life remains. No-one who is living Life or trying to get anything out of Life, but just the beauty and intelligence of Life itself. From here all useful action emerges if necessary, without mental strain.

Part 2 of this book is about functioning in the world without carrying the limiting beliefs and behaviours we have been taught to act on.

Fellow Humans and Interaction

Our interactions are far more harmonious if we bring no expectation to them. If we have no need to be liked, no need to be approved of, no need to be noticed or seen as valuable – then we are natural, and interaction takes care of itself.

Other people exist for us mainly as concepts. We think about them, and assign them a particular mental image. The cage does this, the ego does this. If the ego is in operation, it strongly believes in the separation between me, he and she. If the inner cage is not there, if you allow others to *be* without labeling them, you see they are all yourself in varying forms.

What is untrue is that which differs between people – name, shape, form, personality. What is true – awareness – is one.

Other people are gurus in disguise. Whenever someone else upsets you, it is not personal – they are showing you the cage that lives on in you unnoticed. Others are sometimes needed so you can watch the inner cage shake, and allow it to happen without identifying.

Are you a person, or is the inner person merely an appearance, a thought/image? The inner person sees other persons everywhere. Consciousness sees itself everywhere.

Don't be afraid to be silent around others. Let words emerge from silence if necessary.

If you are around someone who simply cannot stop talking, don't feel like you need to engage. Often these people are energy-sappers; they feed off of your attention. You can later feel drained since your energy has been sucked into their mind and stories. It is the cage of the mind speaking through them, searching for energy.

Let them talk, but you need not be dragged along by meaningless words. They may wake up, or they may get upset since their own cage is not being supported. Let this be, you are not the author of anyone else's inner state.

Are you the one who can't stop talking? Do you find yourself constantly trying to fill the silence with anything that comes to mind? Do your mental commentaries and opinions dominate conversations? The mind has taken over. Watch it act out, observe it with dispassion.

Presence when interacting with others is difficult if there is no presence when not around others. Take moments when you are undisturbed and alone to be surrendered, silent and empty, not wanting or asking for anything, just being, with action taking place or not.

People often want to define you. Their minds want to make a mental image of you and call that "you". Watch this happen, it is quite funny, and does not affect you at all.

Also be aware of your mind trying to define and judge others. Again, it is quite funny, harmless when observed neutrally.

Whatever definition someone has of you is not true. You can not be defined by any word or concept. Judgments from your mind or from others are meaningless.

Shyness or lack of confidence are not things that need to be overcome. We are so conditioned in assertiveness that it places unnecessary pressures on people. Instead of fighting shyness or insecurity, you need not feel a victim. Allow these traits to be as they are. Watch them act out from a surrendered viewpoint. Then if they no longer serve you, they will not stay for long.

Despite your efforts, you can not control what someone else thinks of you. So let it be.

Other people's opinions of you are nothing to do with you. Personal judgements are only mental images. You are not an image or a thing to be judged. Let people judge and be free of it. It does you no harm.

Realise fully that in fact, whatever anyone says or thinks about you, is not actually about you. It is about their own minds. It is not your burden to bear. Everything that someone else seems to judge about you, is purely a creation of their own mind, which is nothing to do with you. In the same way, whenever you judge someone else, it is nothing to do with the truth of another being, it is just a creation of your own mind. When it comes to the truth of each other, we can say nothing that is a real representation.

Be aware of any inner need to judge or condemn others. The tendency of the cage is to often enhance the sense of "otherness", and to inject it with superiority or inferiority. Watch this tendency, but give it no belief.

Whenever someone gives you true, helpful advice, you need not think. You already know it to be true. If someone's words do not resonate in your being, they are probably not worth taking seriously.

Most people will want you to or expect you to conform to the general consensus or way of living. Don't rebel for the sake of it, but don't be guided by the person in the head. Be guided by *being*, by intuition, by spontaneity.

The nature of the mind is to judge, to form opinions and images. Therefore don't expect people to not judge you, or to accept you for who you are. Don't expect anything from them. Accept yourself as you are. Then you are free.

If we believe we have flaws in our character, in the way we act or the way we behave, if someone says "accept yourself" - this does not make sense to our conditioned mind. We are trained to think that improvement can never come through acceptance, it can only come from resistance. The opposite is true. Acceptance is the ground for all useful change, and can make changes in character without effort. You may find that any undesirable character traits are based on a form of resistance. Acceptance undoes this resistance, and therefore also undoes the undesirable trait. We have been taught to never accept ourselves, to always expect ourselves to be "better" or "different". Go the other way, accept yourself without reservation, and see what happens.

That which fears other people is only the ego. Be aware of this fearful inner person, observe it, and see it is not who you are.

The need to justify oneself or defend a certain point of view is wasted energy. What is true needs no defence.

Do not take words too seriously. The opinions and values of

others may well be deluded or dysfunctional. Often people cannot even hear themselves speaking – it is as if they are sleepwalking. What words are useful for you will naturally take root when you take words with less seriousness.

Trying to control others is an exhausting experience. It is also largely unsuccessful. See what it is like to wish to control no one, and instead accept them as they are.

What other people say or do is not really your business. Even what you say or do is not your business. Watch it happen. We can spend so much energy thinking about actions of someone else, or judging someone a certain way, when it actually serves no useful purpose other than to make us feel separate from them.

The mind sucks the Life out of interaction. It turns Life into concepts, so we cannot see things as they are. Real Life is non-conceptual. Get used to looking and perceiving without interpreting or naming anything.

Leave interaction to Life. You need not worry about what you will say or do. Leave it to the spontaneity of Life itself. Be empty.

To judge someone or their actions correctly, you would need extensive knowledge of their thought processes, inner state, all "events" preceding the present moment, and also all "events" that will follow. You would also have to know what the purpose of the world is, and you would have to be sure that all of this knowledge was true. Therefore, we cannot correctly judge anyone or anything as truly good or bad.

The pain that comes with worrying about how others perceive you, is a direct sign that it is not your concern. When you make it your concern, it hurts, and so it is like a dog biting you, saying "keep away!".

What others think of you is not under your control, despite any effort made. Therefore, leave it alone.

The "you" that others judge and label, is a misunderstanding of what you are. Judgements are in the realm of concepts. You are not a concept, so where is the validity of any concern?

Worrying about how others perceive you comes from a deluded self-importance. It is not real. Do you know how small the body is in comparison to the universe? Does the body care how it is perceived? Does awareness care how it is perceived? No. So what does care? It is the false, illusory entity of the mind that thinks it is a body, and cares how it is perceived, since it fears destruction from the judgments of others. See that it is unreal, just a dream.

Be finished with trying to impress anyone. We are trained to impress others from a young age, be it at school or at home – as if you are of higher value if you can impress people or receive praise. Forget all of that.

The tendency to impress or seek approval may still operate. Just watch it casually without giving your belief to it. It is only an old conditioned behaviour. It is not who you are.

Not only does this allow you to feel free, it also means action is far more effective, since the ego can no longer get involved.

If you don't judge others, then their judgements won't mean anything to you.

To be free, give other people freedom to *be*.

What you withhold from others, you withhold from yourself. Find the point of separation between you and the rest of the world. Where do you end and everything else begins? Perhaps this separation can not be located.

Freedom In Action

Free action is inspired, empty of personal clinging, with power from surrendered attention. It does not carry concern of future or past. It is not action that is infected with fear or resistance. It is not personal, it moves from *Being* rather than from conditioning.

The obsession with activity in society is just a characteristic of the cage. It does not understand stillness, it does not understand "enough", it does not understand the intelligence of nature. The ego is in direct opposition to the truth, and so claims that only constant activity is of value.

Pure being is more important than action. *Being* is the foundation of useful action, is not involved in meaningless activity, and can get things done without effort.

A mantra of the conditioned human mind could be described as: "do do do!". Instead, *be* - and allow the doing to unfold by itself.

"What are you doing?", "what do you do?", "what have you been doing?". The importance of doing and doer-ship should be discarded. Forget it, take the opinion of the world to be some kind of joke. Be. Allow. Surrender. This is the source of any fruitful action.

Peaceful activity can exist when you are not resisting the act of doing, and you are not striving to be elsewhere. How does it feel if you do not treat this moment as only a platform to get you to a better moment?

Surrender so completely as if you have nowhere to go, nowhere to be, nothing to do. Then you are present, clear, at peace. See how action takes on a higher quality from here.

Stillness or presence in itself is supremely powerful. It benefits the whole world. From the egoic eye it seems to be useless, nothing, at best a means to an end. "Your duty is to *be*, and not to be this or that" – as Ramana Maharshi said.

Surrendered consciousness alters the vibrational frequency of yourself and the world, and so the useful actions that come from this need not be a concern.

Most of our activity is to escape from the burden of the mind. Don't be afraid of it. Be with it. Let it be. Be fearless and surrendered. With this approach the mind's hold is weakened without your intention.

If you must do something you don't want to do, such as go to work the next day or engage in some event, if it is inevitable, notice how the resistance or dread help serve no useful purpose. It is only our conditioning to identify with these feelings that drain energy and amplify suffering.

If something is inevitable, such as going to work, see how it feels to surrender, to no longer complain or argue with this moment. Let it be. Not only does this free you from the form of the moment, it also allows for useful change to arise more easily. What you resist, persists.

The most boring or frustrating tasks are some of your greatest opportunities for greater peace. By unconditionally surrendering, offering no resistance, the cage crumbles. It may feel uncomfortable as it dies and cries, but let it happen. It is the doorway to freedom.

The word "work" can have such a heavy, negative connotation. It begins when you are more or less forced to do certain things in school. Don't be dominated by this word. It is only a concept. Be aware that your thoughts about work are only thoughts. They can deceive you. Their power over you is weakened when you allow them without resistance, and are neutrally aware of their appearance and disappearance.

Personal thinking claims to be helpful, but when your identity is mixed with it, it just clogs things up.

You can be inspired or intuitively moved to do something...then a voice says "careful, what if...", "maybe not...". Thinking becomes an interference rather than a tool.

Act from your heart's intuition, not from the person's past. It's much easier and far more effective.

Act purely and fully, without regard for what you will get in return. Then you are free, and your action is also of high quality.

There is no hurry! Everyone wants instant "success". Nature takes its time, and is beyond human understanding. The key to any success is to enjoy the process, the work or action involved. To be in a state of not desiring success, not fearing failure, but working or acting for the joy of it – is the most success-promoting state.

When you act as presence, not attached to the results, the fruits take care of themselves.

When you were a child, you had a natural urge to walk. However, you could not walk the first time you tried. You probably fell many times. Even if it hurt, you were not discouraged from walking. You never thought "I'm never going to walk, maybe I should stop getting up". Falling down never meant anything but to get up again. What other people thought, said or did made no difference. You were naturally moved to walk, yet you did not take it too seriously, setbacks did not upset you. Even the falling down toughened you up. While all this was going on, you never allowed your happiness to be dependent on walking. You were just naturally progressing, enjoying the process, not hurried yet ever persevering. The child is naturally moved to walk, without making it personal, until it is walking.

If ever you feel naturally and sincerely urged to do or discover something whilst with this body, be like the child.

What society calls success and failure is really an illusion. Neither exist in reality. They are just interpretations. They are only thoughts based on limited understanding. Consciousness knows no failure or success, all is part of the greater intelligence, and it is as it is.

What you really are does not know success and failure. Consciousness, *being*, or awareness do not change, and do not even take credit for the actions of the body and mind. Success and failure are only mental creations.

"Success" can strengthen the cage. "Failure" can destroy it. Perhaps failure is a greater blessing than we realise. However it can only diminish the cage if you surrender, if you offer no resistance to what the moment presents. This does not mean you do not persevere in action, it just means you are at peace instead of upset.

We always act like failure is to be avoided, failure is bad, failure means you are no good. Perhaps this is another of the school system's most insane yet potent teachings. Forget both failure or success. Both are illusory, both are transient. Act in freedom!

The idea of success has dominated our society. Everyone is obsessed with success, with more. This is largely because we feel invalid, or as if we are somehow lacking, and we want the idea of success to fill this gap. We are also trained from a young age, often to believe that success in working life is the very purpose of Life itself. As if we are here to have a good job and then die. This was certainly my experience – many years were spent in hard and dedicated preparation for the ultimate goal: "a good job", to "be successful".

Get off this bandwagon. Don't be a beggar any longer. This obsession with success not only breeds dependence, misery and constant ups and downs, but it also pushes success away. Attachment to outcomes and "success" means that your action is always tainted. Without expectation, you act more fully, more purely, and naturally action is more effective.

We approach success in a strange and insane way. We are taught success = happiness. Success makes one feel happy since the background feelings of lack or "low worth" of the cage are temporarily alleviated when success occurs. Be aware of any energy in you that claims success will make you happy, and that you can not be happy now. Be alert, feel the energy within the body, be aware of feelings of heaviness or lack, then let it all be. Watch the feelings and allow them. This helps to release and dissolve the heaviness that masks natural contentment beyond success or failure.

If success makes you happy, this is fine, but it will not last, and also means that failure will make you unhappy. Both are disturbances to natural peace and contentment. Don't make personal success the goal of your life, unless you feel it truly helps you. By all means act, do as you feel, but with your dependence on the end result and what you will get, you will be wasting energy, and will always be trapped in the success/failure bondage.

If you find yourself desiring success or fearing failure, this is neither "right" nor "wrong". Never condemn yourself. As with anything else, simply notice and allow these tendencies. Feel their energy. Let them *be* but do not identify with them. Then what is useful remains, and what is useless dissolves, by itself. You will find that any unhelpful fears or desires will be transmuted into higher forms of energy when this approach is adopted.

Success and failure only apply to the ego. Without the little person in the head taking charge of the Life, there is no-one to succeed or fail in the first place. All the work is that of universal intelligence, happening quite spontaneously. Success then takes on a deeper meaning. Rather than success being in what is achieved or gained, success is in the work itself. Presence, perfection in each movement. Work is no longer a means to an end. As a by-product, work takes on a higher quality, and is bound to have more "successful" results.

What is so attractive about the idea of success is a sense of fullness, wholeness, a sense of not needing anything else, a sense that you need not strive any longer or look to some future moment for fulfillment. Success makes happy because in that moment, the cage dissolves. Pure, unapologetic presence emerges, and is fully allowed. For a while, the mind is not justified in saying "but there is something else you need".

This presence and wholeness, which is the true meaning of success, is available here and now. No longer believe in the mind that tells you fulfillment is just round the corner, when the next thing is achieved. Throw out these lies. Relinquish resistance. Simply be aware of yourself, be aware that the mind and body's movements have a force and intelligence of their own. Drop your expectations of the world, and allow your attention to rest as the stillness within, which is unaffected by externals such as success or failure.

If there is a gap in you, a feeling of emptiness that is seeking to be filled, go deeply into this gap. It is in fact peace, stillness, fullness, perhaps covered by a surface layer of fear. This gap is what the ego fears most. Merge with it.

Success in working life is to enjoy, to allow work to be a vehicle for consciousness to express. Consciousness is not concerned with what can be received, it only gives. Then the needs of the body are naturally taken care of. Even with a "boring job" – through acceptance, each movement can become perfect – picking up the phone, writing something down, sitting in a chair. Give up your demands. Let the moment *be*. This is success. Rather than it being the job you hate, it becomes your spiritual practice that demolishes the cage of your mind. You may stay at the job or leave it – things will happen more easily and naturally when you are no longer resisting Life.

If we have a task to complete, often we can become weighed down with the thoughts of "everything I have to do" before the task is completed. The mind creates a burden. It seeks freedom from its own burden by saying: "once everything is done, I can be free". This is a trick. The mind itself is the burden, not the work to be done.

If you place more value on the outcome of activity than you do on the activity itself, there will always be a strain, a searching for a future moment, and as a result the present action will be compromised.

See that whatever happens, whatever will be achieved, it will always be Now. The Now does not change, only the content changes. There is no lasting happiness in content, so don't be a slave to it. Be aware that of all the things the mind will say about what has to be done - such as how difficult or time consuming it will be - action can only occur Now. What action is occurring Now? Only one simple thing, such as writing a word, reading a word, pushing a vacuum, walking down a corridor, driving a car, picking something up - just a simple thing. This is all that can happen - nothing really difficult can happen in the Now - difficulty lies in time and thinking, fantasising about all that needs to be done. The reality is simple - only one thing is being done, which is usually not very difficult.

A common fear is that if we don't have the "security of a job", or are not earning money, we will become beggars on the street. This fear is planted inside us from society and actually originates inside us, to make it appear as if this is the truth of how the world works. The world is a reflection of your mind, not the other way round. Your beliefs create the rules, not the other way round.

One of the reasons this "beggar image" can be a potent fear is that the ego is itself a beggar. Something inside of us resonates with this image of a suffering, lacking, needy prisoner of the world and circumstance, the disconnected victim of an uncaring universe. The ego is constantly begging for more experiences, more money, more security, more pleasure, less pain. The inner beggar dwells within. It fears exposure, and will do everything to cover up its own existence - by preoccupying itself with externals. Watch the inner beggar, and cut him loose without effort. It is not real, give it no belief when it speaks and fears.

The same intelligence that runs the body, regenerates cells, maintains breathing, allows space for thinking, can also run your whole Life. You just have to surrender to it. Feel it. Stop taking the role of God on your own head - trying to work everything out and control everything. If you stop trying to feel safe by arranging circumstances a certain way - then you become aware of an inner safety, beyond the material world, which then has space to emerge and influence your material life.

That is not to say there is anything wrong with getting a job or earning money. These are fine, enjoy. Without the prison of fearful thinking, things will be lighter, less serious, more enjoyable, and action can be even more effective. Since you resonate at a higher frequency, and are in tune with the pure intelligence of Life, you will likely find things working out more harmoniously, without so much effort on your part.

Free From Strain – Effective Meditation

Never let meditation be the chore the mind tries to make it. Meditation is not mental. It has nothing to do with thinking or achieving. It is not the mind's domain.

Let it be a relaxation, a relinquishment of strain and effort, a chance to lay the tensions of ambition and person-hood to one side. A chance to no longer run from anything or seek anything else. Be with what *is*, and be aware of yourself, being.

Don't call it meditation. Don't try to reach anywhere or find anything. Be as you are. Have no expectations. Allow, surrender to this moment and the thoughts, emotions and sensations that come with it. You are purely awareness of all, not an object or a person.

The intention to reach some other point or experience, robs meditation of its joy and of its value. Relinquish personal ambitions, simply surrender and *be*.

Meditation is not only for a certain part of the day. Bring it into all of life. Be with each breath, each movement, aware of thought movements but not disturbed by them. Not judging but allowing, flowing with life and living as inner freedom. The effect this has on the outer life, as a by-product, can also be profound.

"I meditate" or "I am a mediator" can be a huge hindrance to freedom. Give up your identity, let meditation *be*, but claim no ownership or doer-ship. Sit without holding the identity of being "a meditator".

Don't force anything. If you don't feel like meditating, just fully be with this feeling. Often the mind does not want to face its demise. Be with the restlessness or resistance fully, allow it, see how it feels.

Meditation is most effective when it is not used as a means to an end. Often the ego can infiltrate, calling it "my practice", and use it as a tool to get something – more peace, freedom, a clearer head, better ideas etc. Be extreme and use it to get nothing. Let it be, let it act as it wishes. You may find, as a paradox, its effects become greater and more effortless.

We tend to give the mind far too much importance. Without knowing it, people can meditate and yet make meditation totally dependent on the mind – dependent on thoughts or lack of them, trying to get "my mind" to be silent, cherishing no-mind and then suffering the mind state. Don't depend on your mind. Let it be, don't act like you need it to be any particular way.

Being has nothing to do with the mind. A common misconception is that meditation is very mental and mind-based. Forget your mind! Notice the fascination with mind content and then be done with it. Switch to feeling. *Feel* the life in the body, *feel* the sense of presence, space or emptiness. This is *being*.

One of the most simple and effective meditations: disregard all else, surrender all resistance and efforts, and only be aware of the breath.

The breath is always here and now. Simply being aware of it, without making any effort or trying to work anything out, is enough. Awareness of breath means that even if thought or emotion is playing, your attention is not absorbed by it. Your connection with the energy of the body and your own being is then felt far more easily.

The mind will throw up tricks at first, saying that the breath is too simple, or it is boring, or there must be more. These are lies. The mind will likely resist at all costs. To take you away from the breath it may even create feelings of anger, anxiety or frustration. Allow this without judgement. Just stay aware of the breath without expectation, that is all. The mind and personality may be felt as dense energy fields – fine – just be aware of the breath. Be aware of the breath whether sitting or engaged in some activity. It will even enhance effectiveness of action.

Another effective meditation is to simply disregard all shapes, names and forms, and allow the root of your attention to be "I AM" - the sense that you are awake or conscious, the sense that you exist, the sense of *being* or presence. Simply be aware of yourself at the deepest level, before conditioning was placed on the mind. *Feel* who you are before the world gave you an identity, without carrying expectation. Allow the mind to merge in this so that the identity is no longer thought as "I am this or that", but rather the feeling remains - I AM.

Be aware that whatever is perceived, whatever experience there is - this experience is observed. Something is aware of experience coming and going. This is what you are.

If you sit down to meditate with the intention to be free or to know yourself, the person sitting down to meditate is not who you are. Believing you are this entity who claims to be un-free, is the reason for our apparent bondage.

If you wish your inner state to be different, you create an internal conflict. The mind has come in with its opinions and preferences. This is no longer meditation. Instead of wanting the inner energies to be different, act as if you want them to be as they are.

Rather than treating meditation as an exercise to stop your thoughts or "reach" stillness, don't see it as anything. Don't try to get anywhere or achieve anything. Fully allow your inner state to be as it is without trying to change it, and without believing it should be different. Then see what happens.

Questions for meditation: Who are you without the body? Who are you without the mind?

Silence is always here, without anyone trying to keep or maintain it. It is effortless. The mind then comes in with its habitual efforts to seek, think and discover. This effort is so habitual and engrained, that the mind then claims that it takes effort to be silent. This is madness of the mind! Be aware that the person making effort to be still, silent or at peace is the mind itself. Being aware of "the effort-maker" allows you to be yourself, the effortless awareness, one with the silence that is always here, that need not be maintained, kept or held by anyone.

OUT OF THE CAGE AND INTO NATURE

The cage has separated humans from the harmony and oneness of nature. Resume your connection with Life by being aware of nature and its harmony in action.

We tend to think of nature as separate from ourselves. We see nature as having a harmony that is unlike the harmony that exists in humans. To an extent, this is true. The workings of the cage are far less harmonious than that of mother nature. And yet we are still an inextricable part of nature. Let your mind get out of the way – this is what creates disharmony. Allow spontaneity and intuition to run your life, the natural way, when you are no longer believing in the mind and mental conditioning.

A bird does not call itself a bird, a tree does not call itself a tree.

Learn from the animals, from plants, from the Earth. What is the tree worried about? Is the cat regretting what it did yesterday? Is the bird upset about its life situation? Everything is as it is.

Feel your connection with the Earth. Be aware of the Earth beneath your feet, and how huge it is in comparison to the human body. The Earth is the foundation of the body. Without the Earth the body could not *be*. Re-establish this sacred connection, simply by being aware of the Earth beneath you. Gratitude will come naturally.

The stillness of a flower, the energy of a tree, the emptiness of space – be aware of these things without strain, without trying to force anything.

External space does not complain about what arises in it. It lets everything *be*, it treats everything the same. Be like this space. Where is the separation between you and this space? The separation is only a thought or sensation of identity – it is not real.

An acorn grows into a tree without strain, without strategy, without planning. It is a natural unfolding. Allow your own life to unfold in this way.

Ants and bees aren't fascinated with their own personalities. Their identity is with the whole group. They act as one. Let your personality only be used by the Life force spontaneously, when required. Don't be obsessed by it, what's the point? You are not the personality, you are before it.

The ocean does not mind if the surface is still or turbulent. You are the ocean, the mind is the surface – so don't be fascinated with the waves when you are the ocean itself. Be aware of the whole ocean! Then the waves take care of themselves.

On Death and Impermanence

We tend to take things so seriously, but one day all that we perceive, will be gone. In fact it disappears every night when we sleep. The impermanence of all things, when realised and accepted, reveals that what we believe to be so personal and important, actually is not. At all.

At the same time, we can appreciate everything more, since we no longer arrogantly assume it is forever.

What is death? We all talk about it as if we know what it is and what it means. Do you know anything about death for sure? What we fear about death or even the disappearance of the false self, are only thoughts we create about these things. We do not fear the reality of death, but our own ideas about it.

So many of us have an opinion about death – what it means, if it is good or bad. Have you ever experienced it? Do you actually know what it is like to die? If not, then why believe the mind's opinions about something that it knows nothing about?

Since we are eternal, when we become identified with objects and forms, we naturally assume that the things of this moment should not change, and that our bodily life has a certain importance and permanence to it. Most of us live like this material existence is forever, yet we know that it is not. It is only due to confusion of identity. Whatever you can perceive is not permanent. Why should it conform to your mind's wishes, which is itself part of the phenomenal play? That which is aware of all of these things is the permanent, is the real, is what you are.

We confuse our own permanence with the impermanent. Distinguish. What is seen is temporary. Knowing this means the phenomenal world can't command as much seriousness or importance as before, yet it is honoured. What is permanent is no longer ignored.

If you can be aware that all whom you meet are subject to physical death, then there is a shift in what is deemed important. Suddenly what is said or done is not so all-consuming. None of this lasts.

Western culture sees death as some kind of negative, something to feel sorry for, perhaps even a kind of end of freedom. Perhaps the opposite is true. Free from form, perhaps consciousness becomes completely liberated.

That is not to say death is not to be honoured. Yet it may not be as awful as many societies fear.

We tend to think the physical life is the ultimate, something to be clung to and given great seriousness. Perhaps we are completely wrong in assuming this. Who knows what lies beyond? What lies beyond is available here and now through utter allowance of the form of this moment. Then you are taken beyond form, and are aware of your formless nature, not subject to death.

It is easy to see that all things are impermanent. All that you can perceive is transient, including the body and mind. What is not often done is to go deeply into this fact, to contemplate and fully accept that all forms and names must come to an end. What remains, what endures, is no different than your Self.

To fully accept the nature of impermanence, is to go beyond it. When you resist it or remain ignorant of it, you remain trapped.

Don't take life too seriously. Soon all will be gone. Without seriousness, you will enjoy more, attach less, and act more effectively.

Emptying The Collective Cage – Healing The World

The corrupt outer systems that govern societies that many are now rebelling against are built on the ideas of separation, resistance and control. They are systems of the cage. For them to be replaced by a higher society, our inner state must shift from egoic to universal consciousness. If not, then the current system will only be replaced by another similar one. It all rests on our inner state.

If all people rebelled against slavery to thinking, if all beings surrendered their needs to know, understand and constantly think – then a forceful outer rebellion would hardly be needed. Change in society's structures would naturally occur to reflect the collective inner state of humanity.

The help that you give others will be more efficient and natural the more you are surrendered and at peace. Realise your natural presence, and see the dream-like nature of the cage. Whatever your outer purpose to serve humanity may be, however seemingly small or large, it will arise from here. You need not desperately chase after Life to claim that you can help it. Life knows. Your services are given when required, by Life.

We often feel as if we should be making a difference in the world – this is often seen as the ideal life – to make a difference, to help the world. Don't be desperate for this. One who is free of the world can help it more effectively than one who is bound. Be rooted in your being. Life will organize what needs to be done, which may include your natural actions, which come from natural urges. Just remain open and nonjudgemental of Life's plans for you.

Don't be so distracted by what you are doing for the world that you ignore your own being. Presence and inner silence benefit all.

Just surrendering resistance or denial of this moment is far more beneficial to the world than you may think. It helps the whole planet when a human is in a peaceful, silent or surrendered state.

Since the world and its sufferings sprout from the inner dysfunction of mankind, dissolving your own self-inflicted suffering is perhaps your finest service to the world.

Don't be obsessed with action and ignore your inner state. Maintain some attention in *being*, in space, in emptiness. This is the foundation of all useful action – be it visible or invisible.

Never blame society. You can be aware of its falsities, but to play the blame game only keeps you in conflict and resistance. Society is mostly sick. Heal it by being your Self, by being guided by the infinite and not the cage.

If you *try* to love people, if you *try* to be compassionate, you can get into a mess. Don't force anything. Be natural. Be empty, open and surrendered. All real love and compassion arise naturally from here, without any personal effort or intention.

The world is full of noise. To heal it, be aware of silence. Inner or outer silence – same thing. Give less fascination to content and be more aware of space. Overlook form and be the formless. These things help the world tremendously.

Many of the world's griefs come from fear, which leads to an obsession with control. Relinquish control of your life. Even if you can only manage this partially at first, you will notice a greater ease, lightness and harmony in events. Relax, let Life support you rather than feeling as if you are struggling alone.

Let calls to action come from *being*, from existence, rather than the little scared voice in the head. This scared person doesn't even exist, it is only imagined.

In the same way that outer political systems need your belief to survive, so does the inner controller we call the ego. They are part of the same thing. Transcend the root – the "Imaginary Me" – by hearing it without labeling it, or by searching for it to see if it is actually real.

The more we react to political systems and affirm "we are not free" – the more we feel trapped. Rather than always fighting against the old, let the new emerge by itself. No longer believe in the old ways of thinking, the ways of resistance, fear, time, lack and separation. No longer believe in the mind that is constantly looking for the "next thing" or for "something else". Give up looking elsewhere for peace, give up trying to change yourself.

Be as you are. Your actions in the world will take on a revolutionary quality from here, and your state of consciousness alone will affect the planet for the better. There is nothing wrong with awareness raising, campaigns, petitions, protests etc., be involved with these if you feel moved to. But without the carrying an inner state of conflict, of "us vs them", you will no longer strengthen the apparent evils of the world.

Final Words

Forget the ways of thinking that the world seems to have given you. No longer be hard on yourself, be empty of expectation and resistance. Give in, surrender, and let all action emerge naturally from here. Let intuition be your guide, give less importance to the voice in the head. Don't contribute to any inner energy that makes you suffer.

Fully realise that who you have been told you are – an individual, a person born on a certain date at a certain time, someone with certain characteristics – is not who you are. This individual personal identity is only an idea in the mind. When believed in, it gives rise to the cage of personal thinking and suffering. Be aware of yourself beyond the idea of the person, feel yourself as the intelligence, the space in which the inner person and body arises and plays. Relax, there is no need for strain in all of this. Strain and personal effort are the very hindrances in themselves. Do not identify yourself to be any self-image, or any thing you can perceive.

Be aware of who you are at the deepest level, without needing to add concepts to yourself. When it comes to who you are, don't take anyone's word for truth. Feel it for yourself. Let go of all names and labels, including the "spiritual names" such as "awareness" or "consciousness". Simply *be*.

The person that feels internally trapped, is only an image that arises in you. You are that in which the trapped sensation has arisen. You are out of the cage.

Thank you for purchasing this book. I hope it has served, and perhaps continues to serve a useful purpose in your experience. Even though it is described as "the cage", never treat your mind as an enemy. When it creates suffering, it is merely showing you not to identify with it. The troubles it creates are merely indicators that it is not real or worthy of trust.

If you feel the book has benefitted you, please take a moment to leave a review on the book's Amazon page for others to see. Thank you.

ALSO AVAILABLE

Undisturbed: A Guide To Emotional Wellness

Summary:

"A book designed to dispel the myths we have about emotions, and how to treat them in such a way that they no longer become a burden...

We are often faithful to emotions, feeling somehow owned by them, when in fact emotions depend on us. We need not cling to them or take them so seriously. They are energy movements, which would not exist if we were not here to witness them.

This book aims to show that we need not label our emotions in any way. We need not regulate or police ourselves. We can relinquish suppressing something because we believe it is "wrong" to feel a certain way – this is all just conditioning. We can stop distinguishing between good and bad emotions, right or wrong feelings, feelings "I should have" or "should not have", what is "spiritual" or "not spiritual", and instead return to pure experience, which is untarnished by story-telling, resistance or personal attachment.

From here we become aware of the deeper peace available prior to emotional movement, where emotions can not stick, which is also the source of all useful action."

TO CONTACT ADAM, OR FOR MORE INNER PEACE RESOURCES AND FREE CONTENT, YOU CAN VISIT HIS WEBSITE:
WWW.INNERPEACENOW.COM

Printed in Great Britain
by Amazon